The Little Book of

Big

Reasons
to Homeschool

The Little Book of

BIG
Reasons
to Homeschool

David & Kim d'Escoto

B&H
PUBLISHING GROUP

Nashville, Tennessee

ISBN: 978-0-8054-4484-1

Published by B&H Publishing Group,
Nashville, Tennessee

Dewey Decimal Classification: 371.042
Subject Heading: HOME SCHOOLING

1 2 3 4 5 6 7 8 9 10   10 09 08 07

To our five "Big Reasons"
Kayla, Nathaniel, Celia, Marisa, and Ava
and any future "little reasons" the Lord may bring
to our family.
We love you so much!

Contents

The Anvil—God's Word

Last eve I passed beside a blacksmith's door,
And heard the anvil ring the vesper chime;
Then, looking in, I saw upon the floor
Old hammers, worn with beating years of time.

"How many anvils have you had," said I,
"To wear and batter all these hammers so?"
"Just one," said he, and then, with twinkling eye,
"The anvil wears the hammers out, you know."

And so, thought I, the anvil of God's Word,
For ages skeptic blows have beat upon;
Yet, though the noise of falling blows was heard,
The anvil is unharmed—the hammers gone.

—Author Unknown

Acknowledgments

The following people have been instrumental in our lives and throughout the many phases of this project, and to them we are very grateful: Steve Quinn—for giving of your time and talents from the beginning of this endeavor and for being a devoted brother in Christ. May the Lord continue to bless the work of your hands. Rob and Daphne Vance—for your encouragement, wisdom, and contagious enthusiasm. It was "huge"! May God continue to bless your family in your homeschool journey. Scott and Shelly Schuler—for your gracious hearts, invaluable insight, and perseverance. May your family reap many fruits as you obey the Lord's calling to homeschool. Liam and Kristin Connolly—for your timely input and support. We look forward to sharing many family adventures in the years ahead. May the Lord continue to hold you in the palm of His hand. Our parents—for laying the foundations of our faith. We hope to continue this legacy of faithfulness for your grandchildren, great-grandchildren, and generations to come. Jane Decort—for being there at the beginning to share with us the homeschool vision with grace and wisdom. The pioneers of the homeschool movement—for boldly and courageously paving the way for the rest of us. Zan Tyler, David Webb, and the wonderful people at B&H Publishing Group—for your support and vision. And most importantly, God—for salvation through Your Son, Jesus Christ, and for Your Word, the "Anvil" for all generations.

Preface

Homeschooling wasn't something we had always planned on doing. With Kim's bachelor's degree in elementary education and a few years of teaching under her belt prior to motherhood, we didn't even think about schooling our own at home. We believed that children should be educated by professionals, the supposed authorities on education. The homeschool families we met now and then were nice, but we automatically categorized them as being, well, different. Maybe they had bad experiences in public schools and couldn't afford Christian schools, we reasoned. Perhaps they were fear-driven, overly protective parents who refused to let their children out into the real world. Or, maybe they were rebels who wanted to make some kind of political statement. OK, the term *religious zealots* also came to mind. Whatever the case, we figured homeschoolers were a scattered few, treading off the beaten path into the unknown. Eventually, they would probably come around and see that schools were where children belonged.

Unlike Paul in his rampage against the early Christians, we weren't out to persecute anyone. However, we did experience a similar, unpredictable about-face in our convictions. Part of the revelation came with the unsettling feeling we faced when the time approached to send our firstborn off to first grade, knowing this full-day arrangement would take her from our nest longer than she had ever been before, as a part-time preschooler and kindergartner. Was it already time to delegate to another such a large portion of her training and nurturing? Our apprehension grew stronger as we questioned school board politics, policy changes, and a few ugly scandals. But the biggest factor that drew us to keep our children home wasn't as much the frustration and dissatisfaction with the current school arrangement as it was a sudden awakening and attraction toward the perfect alternative—homeschooling.

The Lord brought Jane, a dear woman of faith and a seasoned homeschool veteran, into Kim's life at just the right time. Through her friendship, words of wisdom, encouragement, and prayers, we began to understand homeschooling in a new way. Meeting her close-knit family and admiring the special relationship they shared sparked a greater desire to investigate this option. A timely visit to our wonderful state homeschool convention preceded lots of reading and research, and we soon became convinced that this was the right path for our family.

Now we're among the "different" ones. And we love it. In fact, our family has been so blessed by our experience that we are passionate about sharing the homeschool vision. The years have strengthened our conviction that this is the right choice for families who are seeking the blessings of togetherness, richer learning experiences, and a lasting godly legacy.

Many times we have been asked about our lifestyle—by skeptics and seekers alike. It's difficult to share the full vision of homeschooling in a casual conversation at the refreshment table after church or in the waiting room at a child's dance class. We found ourselves wishing we had just the right resource to share a little research and reason behind family-based learning. And while there are many great books out there with loads of information, extensive studies, and specific how-to's by wonderful people in the homeschool community (to whom we are forever grateful for paving the way for newcomers), we struggled to find something complete, yet concise. Unlike some of the heavy, more in-depth titles, we wanted to offer a resource that would be sweet and simple as PIE: Persuade, Inform, and Encourage.

Perhaps you are at a crossroads, and you seek compelling reasons to pursue the path of homeschooling. Maybe you are already homeschooling and wish to pass along facts and figures to curious friends or concerned in-laws. If so, you might find this book to be just what you need for sharing the basics on a sometimes emotionally-heated topic. Or, it could be that you've been traveling on the road of homeschooling for a while and simply desire a little affirmation from some fellow travelers that you are, indeed, on the right path.

Whatever your situation, we hope you'll sink your teeth into this PIE as we share some of the same guidance that we received from other homeschool veterans, along with insight gleaned from our own experience over the years. A companion discussion/Bible study guide is also available on our Web site for your own personal reflection time, home-school support groups, or church Bible studies, enabling you to dig deeper into Scripture and facilitate discussions (see www.dexios.info).

Our prayer is that all who read this book would real-ize that God is truly moving in our world through the homeschool movement. In a time when we have witnessed the fabric of the family becoming unraveled and the grave results on society, He is turning the hearts and minds of children and parents back toward each other, one family at a time. Many can already testify that there are real blessings to being obedient to God's call, blessings that will carry on into eternity.

Blessings in Christ!
David and Kim d'Escoto

And whatever you do, in word or deed,
do everything in the name of the Lord Jesus,
giving thanks to God the Father through him.

COLOSSIANS 3:17

History of Homeschooling

*And these words that I command you today shall
be on your heart. You shall teach them diligently
to your children, and shall talk of them when you sit
in your house, and when you walk by the way, and when
you lie down, and when you rise. You shall bind them
as a sign on your hand, and they shall be as frontlets
between your eyes. You shall write them on the doorposts
of your house and on your gates.*

DEUTERONOMY 6:6–9

History shows that today's home education movement
actually springs from a rich heritage of family-based
learning. Through the centuries, beginning with the earli-
est recorded history found in the Holy Bible, the practice of
many cultures worldwide reflected the belief that parents

and immediate family members should be the primary educators of children.

God-fearing people from the very beginning knew, as Scripture points out, that children are a gift from God and that He delegates to parents the authority to "bring them up in the discipline and instruction of the Lord" (Ephesians 6:4). This responsibility was taken seriously, not as a suggestion, but a command from God. Just as there are consequences to ignoring His commands, there are also rewards for being obedient to them, such as one stated in the book of Proverbs: "Train up a child in the way he should go; even when he is old he will not depart from it" (Proverbs 22:6).

While this is not a guarantee that our children will follow the Lord, it is filled with wisdom and incentive toward raising children with propriety and purpose. When studying the lives of our forefathers, we can see how seriously this guideline was taken.

American Roots

American history shows that in the seventeenth and eighteenth centuries, when this country's founders were firmly rooted in biblical principles, parents were the primary teachers of their children. Education was not the responsibility of the government. Moral values, reading, writing, computation skills, and eventually some sort of vocational training were the main emphases in the early American homeschools.

The Bible was the primary textbook in most homes and served as the motivation for acquiring literacy skills.

Prior to compulsory education, findings show that the literacy rate in America was as high as 90 to 98 percent,[1] a remarkable level that has never been attained since the establishment of our current state-controlled education system. A recent survey revealed the drastic decline in U.S. literacy: 21 to 23 percent, or some 40 to 44 million of the 191 million adults in the United States, demonstrated incompetence in the lowest level of reading, writing, and mathematical skill.[2]

Today, literacy has been redefined to mean a mere squeaking by in the basics of reading, writing, and math skills. Historically, the standards were much higher. Consider the *Appleton School Reader*, compiled of original prose by authors like William Shakespeare, Henry Thoreau, George Washington, Sir Walter Scott, Mark Twain, Benjamin Franklin, Oliver Wendell Holmes, Daniel Webster, Lewis Carroll, Thomas Jefferson, and Ralph Waldo Emerson. In 1882, this was average fifth-grade reading material.[3] Today, one in five high school graduates cannot even read his or her diploma.[4]

> *More than ninety years have gone by since Dewey set American education on its progressive course. The result is an educational system in shambles, a rising national tide of illiteracy and social misery caused in its wake.*
>
> SAMUEL BLUMENFELD,
> *The Blumenfeld Education Letter*

Even when the idea of formal schooling started to grow during the nineteenth century, this was still controlled largely by the parents. Most children who attended grammar schools at age eight or nine already had substantial skill in reading and writing, previously developed at home. Formal book learning was only a small piece of the educational puzzle. Life skills, homemaking, and biblical values were still a priority and took place naturally in the home, where parents fared quite well as teachers of their children.

Home Educated Hall of Fame

It is encouraging to know that some of our country's most influential people were educated at home, including presidents, inventors, scientists, writers, artists, ministers, and businessmen. The following are just a few names that might ring a bell.

To begin with, there are those "Mount Rushmore Guys": George Washington, Thomas Jefferson, Abraham Lincoln, and Theodore Roosevelt. Their mothers and fathers probably never imagined that the faces of their little boys would someday be carved on the side of a mountain, becoming a national monument to four of the most influential men in our nation's history.

Add to that impressive line-up a few more good men, and women: James Madison, John Quincy Adams, John Tyler, William Henry Harrison, Franklin D. Roosevelt, and Woodrow Wilson. How about Benjamin Franklin and

Patrick Henry? There's also Jonathan Edwards, Dwight L. Moody, Robert E. Lee, Stonewall Jackson, George Patton, Douglas MacArthur, and Booker T. Washington. Thomas Edison had actually attended public school but was expelled because his teacher said his mind was "addled." So Mrs. Edison taught young Tom at home where he says, "She instilled in me the love and purpose of learning."[5]

Some notable home educated women include Martha Washington, Abigail Adams, Mercy Warren, Florence Nightingale, Phillis Wheatley, Clara Barton, Pearl S. Buck, and Agatha Christie.

Other writers and artists joining the ranks of homeschoolers include Mark Twain, George Bernard Shaw, Andrew Wyeth, and Irving Berlin, who quit school in second grade and became a self-taught musician. There is also Ansel Adams, the renowned photographer, who credits his father for recognizing his special needs that were not being met in public schools. He was pulled out of school, thus reviving what he calls "an internal spark tenderly kept alive and glowing by my father."[6]

A few homeschooled hall of fame individuals from abroad include Blaise Pascal, C. S. Lewis, Charles Dickens, Claude Monet, Felix Mendelssohn, Wolfgang Amadeus Mozart, and John Newton, the London preacher and hymn writer of the beloved song *Amazing Grace*.

As you can see, home education, one of our most basic freedoms, has been a blessing to our land, bearing forth a great many leaders. Would our country be where it is today without the properly nurtured hearts and minds of so many distinguished individuals, including men and women of faith, who forged our Constitution and fought for freedoms so often taken for granted?

Waning

Homeschooling was successful and prevalent not only in the United States but in many nations until the middle to late nineteenth and early twentieth centuries. At that time, the idea of "common schools" was born, schools attended in common by all children, where a common political and social ideology was to be taught. Eventually, the belief evolved that trained professionals could best carry out the goals of the state, and public education as we know it was established.

Who was instrumental in paving the public school path, and how did the worldviews of these individuals shape their goals? To begin with, there was Horace Mann, considered to be the father of public education. Although claiming to be a Christian, he was a devout Unitarian, a faith that, among many heresies, fundamentally denies the deity of Christ. Furthermore, much of Mann's thinking was steeped in the pseudoscience of phrenology, the study of bumps on people's heads as a gauge of intelligence. According to Mann's ideals, common schools would be responsible for saving society. As the secretary of the Massachusetts Board of Education in 1837, he began his crusade to transform public ideology by reaching and shaping young minds, a responsibility he claimed belonged not to parents, but to the state. This, in turn, led to compulsory school attendance laws. Although Mann argued that the taxpayer should not be required to pay for religious schools, public schools eventually became the channel for the religion of humanism.

Another agenda-pusher in the public education movement was John Dewey, a signer and contributor to *Humanist Manifesto I*—a statement of beliefs that parallels in many ways the ideologies of the *Communist Manifesto*. Humanism discounts absolute truth, regards the universe as self-existing, and rejects the authority of God, replacing it with the belief that man defines his own morality. Believing that man's goals should be centered upon attaining personal fulfillment, the humanist's focus becomes the here and now. Through Dewey's efforts, humanism would become the religion of the schools and public school teachers the "prophets." Claiming that the state can do no wrong and determines what is right, Dewey sought to use the vehicle of public education as social and mental hygiene, whereby traditional values, such as patriotism and reverence to God, would be wiped away.

During this era, humanism found its perfect companion—evolution. Like fuel and fire, these two notions combined to ignite a common philosophy that would be branded into the framework of education. Interestingly, the year Mann died (1859) was the same year in which Dewey was born and Darwin's *Origin of Species* was published.

Darwin's "theory of evolution"—an idea that reduces man to an animal, evolved by chance, and denies the biblical account of creation—soon became a regular component of public school science curriculum. Darwin himself admitted, "I am quite conscious that my speculations run quite beyond the bounds of true science."[7] Nearly one hundred fifty years later, evolution remains an unproven "speculation" full of holes. Nonetheless, it is still taught as fact in schools today.

The basis of our current education system has its roots in an eclectic blend of unbiblical worldviews, injected into the mainstream by men like Mann, Dewey, and Darwin. A few apropos acronyms for remembering their beliefs are: Mann—CATS (Children are the State's), Dewey—HOG (Humans over God), and Darwin—APE (Actively Propagandized Evolution).

Through the stalwart efforts of these men and many others, the purpose of education was altered, and the responsibility once held by parents was released to the state. Once commonplace, American homeschooling dwindled to near-extinction by the mid-1970s. By the late 1970s,

---

I am convinced that the battle for humankind's future must be waged and won in the public school classroom by teachers that correctly perceive their role as proselytizers of a new faith. . . . The classroom must and will become an arena of conflict between the old and new—the rotting corpse of Christianity . . . and the new faith of humanism.

JOHN D. DUNPHY,
Humanist magazine

---

99 percent of school-aged children were attending institutional classroom schools.[8]

Rebirth

The modern homeschool movement is said to have begun in the early 1980s. Today homeschoolers are making history of their own as the numbers continue to rise rapidly. During the 2002–2003 school year, it was estimated that 1.7 to 2.1 million children were being taught at home by their parents.[9] At current growth rates, it is projected that there will be about three million homeschooled students in the United States by the end of the year 2010.[10]

So, why the resurgence of home education? What brought on this recent rebirth of an age-old lifestyle of family-based learning? The rationale that homeschoolers share for reclaiming the privilege and responsibility of teaching their own at home are as individual as the families themselves. Reasons are usually a combination of proactive and reactive ones, such as providing richer academic experiences, minimizing negative social settings, and meeting the special learning needs of their children. By far, the strongest conviction shared by parents is that of instilling in children their faith and values.[11]

Approximately 90 percent of homeschooling families in the United States are Christians,[12] most of whom believe that the Bible is the inerrant Word of God and the basis for absolute truth. In stark contrast to the godless public

> *For we do not wrestle against flesh and blood, but against the rulers, against the authorities, against the cosmic powers over this present darkness, against the spiritual forces of evil in the heavenly places.*
>
> EPHESIANS 6:12

education system, home education is an opportunity for parents to reclaim the role of discipling children, teaching them to shine in the midst of darkness. It can be looked at as a spiritual revival, a wake-up call to a land in serious moral decline. To better understand the vision of homeschooling, we will look at the benefits to the mind, body, and soul.

Benefits to the Mind

Do not be conformed to this world, but be transformed
by the renewal of your mind, that by testing
you may discern what is the will of God, what
is good and acceptable and perfect.

ROMANS 12:2

There are many advantages to sharing life and learning with our children at home. First, let's explore the benefits of the mind—the academic side. Naturally, this is a major concern for people considering the path of homeschooling. We all want our children to be literate, to develop their minds, and to use the gifts with which they have been blessed by their Creator. One of the biggest benefits to homeschooling is being able to put aside ineffective "schoolish ways" and take a more successful, individualized approach to learning.

Uniquely Created

The following passage from the book of Psalms beautifully illustrates how each of us was created as a unique being.

*For you formed my inward parts; you knitted me together
in my mother's womb. I praise you, for I am fearfully
and wonderfully made. Wonderful are your works;
my soul knows it very well. My frame was not
hidden from you,
when I was being made in secret, intricately woven
in the depths of the earth. Your eyes saw my
unformed substance;
in your book were written, every one of them, the days that
were formed for me, when as yet there were none of them.*
PSALM 139:13–16

Our heavenly Father authored a special purpose for each of His children and has given to parents the authority to see that His plan is followed. By homeschooling, we can really tune in to our children's unique qualities, address their individual needs in learning styles, pace, and interests, and encourage them to follow their divine appointments in life.

Learning Styles

At home, parents are able to tailor academics to children's individual learning styles. Ask any number of elementary school teachers and they will probably agree that one of the biggest challenges is meeting the individual needs of twenty-five or more students simultaneously. Since this is nearly impossible, teachers must gear instruction to the average student. Children above or below this level are expected to conform. By contrast, the personalized instruction of homeschooling creates an optimum learning environment for each child, regardless of level.

Learning styles vary distinctly from person to person. Some children learn best through a hands-on approach. Others lean toward an auditory style. And then there are those who prefer a strong visual learning environment. Add to that the list of multiple intelligences, which also include verbal, logical, musical, interpersonal, and intrapersonal abilities. There are so many ways to assess individual learning strengths. Unfortunately, institutional schooling methods tend to capitalize exclusively on verbal and logical skills, leaving many children out of the loop.

> *I have often thought that with eight children I would eventually get two that are the same. I have not. Yes, there may be just four learning styles, but within them are multiples of combinations. So your job as an educating parent is to learn your child.*
>
> TERRI CAMP,
> *Ignite the Fire*

Determining a child's learning preferences takes time as they develop over the years. Can we really expect a classroom teacher to know what is best for our child among a large group in a brief 180-day school year? Parents know their children in an intimate way, far more intimately than a schoolteacher can. The love and appreciation born out of the parent-child relationship fuels the desire to discover our child's unique bent and thus create the optimum learning environment.

Quality Time

The tutorial style of home teaching results in less wasted time. Because teaching at home is one-on-one, parents can get immediate feedback on a child's progress. Meaningful dialogue replaces the need for an overuse of mundane workbooks and worksheets, which teachers too often rely upon as a means of proving that concepts have been learned. With less pencil pushing required, there is more time for enriching activities. And unlike a classroom environment, less time is wasted on disciplinary challenges, class transitions, waiting in line for help, and the many distractions that are inevitable in a large group setting. Therefore, children are better able to concentrate and engage in complex activities and thought processes. As a result, the typical homeschool day is actually much shorter and more productive than an institutional school day. Many families are done with studies in a fraction of the time that most children are sitting in a classroom or a school bus. Some homeschoolers even schedule a four-day week, setting aside the fifth day for field trips or special activities.

A Pace of Their Own

Children develop at different rates and should not be forced to conform to the pace and structure of a one-size-fits-all school system. Without the pressure of feeling left behind or the boredom of being unchallenged, children can work in the home at a comfortable pace. When an area is mastered, they can skip ahead to something new. If a concept needs further reinforcement, this can be addressed until the child is ready to move on.

School readiness is an important issue when considering the needs of a child. The unfortunate trend is to require too much too soon of little ones. Despite the government's push to give children a "Head Start," studies show that many children just aren't ready for the rigors of formal schooling until age eight to ten, when they are better able to handle the physical, mental, and social demands. Dr. Raymond and Dorothy Moore, leaders in homeschool and Christian education, point out:

> The sequence for the average child these days often spells disaster for both mental and physical health in a sure sequence: 1) *uncertainty* as the child leaves the family nest early for a less secure environment, 2) *puzzlement* at the new pressures and restrictions of the classroom, 3) *frustration* because unready learning tools—senses, cognition,

brain hemispheres, coordination—cannot handle the regimentation of formal lessons and the pressures they bring, 4) *hyperactivity* growing out of nerves and jitter, from frustration, 5) *failure* which quite naturally flows from the four experiences above, and 6) *delinquency* which is failure's twin and apparently for the same reason.[1]

Setting a slow and steady pace in the warmth of the home makes education much less stressful and lays a positive foundation for the child's future.

Freedom from Labels

Forcing early school entrance and unnatural performance expectations actually backfires into burnout, creating an epidemic of diagnoses from a growing list of labels like learning disabled (LD), behavior disorder (BD), emotional disorder (ED), attention deficit disorder (ADD), attention deficit hyperactivity disorder (ADHD), and oppositional defiant disorder (ODD), which is pretty S-A-D.

> *But God chose what is foolish in the world to shame the wise; God chose what is weak in the world to shame the strong; God chose what is low and despised in the world, even things that are not, to bring to nothing things that are.*
>
> 1 CORINTHIANS 1: 27–28

Learning disabilities are often misunderstood by the use of labels. As explained by Linda Kane, Neurodevelopmentalist and Sound Therapy Specialist:

Labels do nothing but limit and lower expectations. . . . If opportunities are not offered, often due to the limitations set forth by the self-fulfilling prophecy of the label expectation, less will be achieved. Learning-disability labels are interesting in nature. Most believe they are unchangeable conditions you must learn to live with. They are treated as diseases. The term *disease* gives one the impression that there is nothing you can do to change the situation. . . . Only by addressing the root causal level will freedom from labels, with all their frustrations, pain, and limitations, be achieved.[2]

At an age when a child's delicate self-concept is being formed, the stigma of labels can be a lifelong hindrance to academic growth. Without the pressures of strict grade-level expectations, children can learn with freedom and confidence in the home.

Internal Satisfaction for Learning

At home, an intrinsic desire to learn is developed. Classifications like "slow" or "gifted" can create inferiority or superiority complexes. Classmates will compare, and this is not a good motivator for success. Parents and teachers may view a little "healthy competition" as a good thing, but when children are motivated by superficial rewards and recognition, the true desire to learn is squelched. The survival-of-the-fittest mentality might get results on the surface level, but this has little to do with real growth. And it doesn't take into consideration the needs of the struggling student. Success means different things for each child, something that stars, stickers, and grade-point averages cannot measure. Free from external pressures to perform and superficial motivators, homeschooled children can develop an internal satisfaction for learning, which has lifelong implications.

Multi-age Teaching

At home, curriculum can be tailored to include the whole family. Many subjects, such as history, geography, science, and the Bible, can span multiple age levels. Families often tie subjects together using unit studies. For example, a study on Ancient Egypt can incorporate not only history but also math, art, writing, reading, science, and the Bible.

Brothers and sisters make great teacher's aides by tutoring one another, gaining a sense of pride and satisfaction. Even the smallest family members absorb what is being learned right along with their older siblings. When one of our daughters was barely two, she had heard her older brother and sister recite the first chapter of Psalms so often that she actually memorized it with them. In her own cute baby talk, she really knew the entire passage. That was a precious moment that is imprinted on our hearts, one of so many that is experienced when we spend quality time learning together each day.

Delight-directed Learning

Delight-directed learning means that lessons and schedules are built upon family members' interests. Rather than becoming captives of the state, homeschool families are able to customize schedules and learning goals. Whether your interests include music, art, science, sports, gardening, or traveling, using your family's interests as a springboard is a great way to customize your curriculum. Special-interest projects and field trips can enrich the experience of education at home. Activities like these bring subjects to life and make learning fun and purposeful.

If you look at the lives of famous homeschooled people and their accomplishments, you will find a common thread. They were able to tap into their personal passions at a young age, instead of being confined to a rigorous school day schedule. Just imagine how many masterpieces in art, music, or literature might have been stifled had the potential of these men and women been limited by an institutional education.

Learning in the Context of Life

Instead of 180 days of school per academic year—the average for public and parochial schools—most home educators can honestly say that learning happens 365 days per year. Topics can be discussed at the dinner table or driving in the car. The pastor's sermon in church might tie in with family Bible readings. Vacations can include trips to historic sites or taking in the beauty of God's creation.

Great literature is read aloud and discussed together. The entire family develops important life skills by cooking, gardening, doing household chores and home improvement projects. Even a new baby's arrival is a precious learning experience and a welcome addition to any curricular plans. Many homeschool families also participate in home-based businesses, ministries, and missionary work. Endeavors such as these offer firsthand preparation for the real world year-round, something that classroom settings just cannot offer.

Parental Example

There's a saying: "Children learn more by what is caught than by what is taught." When parents are excited about learning, their children are too. Rather than limiting mom and dad's involvement to chief lunch maker, chauffeur, and report card signer, homeschool parents are involved first-hand. Instead of getting the typical "Oh, nothing" response to the question "What did you do in school today?" they know and appreciate the scope and sequence of their children's education.

One of the best ways to learn something new is by teaching it. When parents participate in their children's activities, they get a second education right along with them, setting a wonderful example and fostering a true love for learning that lasts a lifetime. We are continually amazed at how much we are learning with our children as we explore our interests together.

The Bible teaches us that we are each created in a special way, comparing us to clay at the hand of the Potter. We are not made from the same mold or evolved by chance but are artistically formed and fashioned throughout life, according to God's distinct purpose for each of us. It is our responsibility as parents to seek the will of the Father as instruments in the molding and shaping of our children.

Like Michelangelo, who regarded the masterpiece within the stone and said, "I saw the angel in the marble and carved until I set it free," God sees the potential in each of us. By embracing the special role that our own families play in tailoring our children's education, we are setting our children free to rise to their unique calling in life.

> *But now, O LORD, you are our Father; we are the clay, and you are our potter; we are all the work of your hand.*
> ISAIAH 64:8

Creativity and Intellectual Growth

We've all heard the saying "The mind is a terrible thing to waste." Upon looking at the results being produced by the public school system, one has to wonder how much potential is being lost each year. An estimated 21 million Americans simply cannot read, which translates to $225 billion a year in lost productivity, among other tragedies.[3] Fully 85 percent of unwed mothers and 70 percent of Americans who get arrested are illiterate.[4] Home education can raise the bar of achievement in a variety of ways. How is this accomplished?

Out of the Box

Through homeschooling, subjects can be taught outside the institutional box of today's education system. In mass education, lesson plans are carefully constructed around state-mandated testing requirements. Toward the end of each school year, there is usually a mad rush to get through the textbooks and complete those checklists. The students open their heads and the information is poured in. With an emphasis on memorizing irrelevant facts, it's no wonder so many students fall into the pattern of studying for a test and forgetting the information immediately after taking it.

School materials leave a lot to be desired. Too often, lessons are limited by dry textbooks and workbooks that turn learning into drudgery. Breaking out of the textbook/workbook routine opens a world of possibilities.

Many homeschoolers have embraced the use of "living books," a term used by nineteenth-century educator Charlotte Mason, to describe books that are well-written and engaging. They absorb the reader as the narrative and characters "come alive." Meaningful studies spring forth from great literature, which replaces "twaddle," as Mason dubs the uninspiring, dumbed-down books used in the typical classroom.

The many popular contemporary book series published today and made available on the shelves of most libraries and bookstores has reduced recreational reading to a fare of uninspiring dime-store drivel and questionable pop fiction, for which many of today's youth have acquired an appetite. Why give our children intellectual junk food when we can give them nourishment for their hearts and minds?

On a personal note, my least favorite subject back when I (Kim) was a student is actually now one of our family favorites—history. Through great books and projects, the people and events come to life. The truth behind the character of many Christian heroes of the faith is discovered, truth that is distorted or completely ignored in secular curriculum. I'm probably not alone in feeling a little short-changed by the lack of depth and excitement with which history, and a few other subjects, was presented in my traditional school experience. All that I really recall was a big, boring textbook filled with a series of dates and dry facts to memorize, none of which I even remembered after taking the tests. What's amazing is that a student can ace tests and learn virtually nothing.

> *You went to high school, and after that, college. . . . You learned that history is a collection of meaningless and unintelligible facts, that Christians are behind the majority of the world's problems, and that, when it comes to historical interpretation, intelligence and cynicism are synonyms.*
>
> DOUG PHILLIPS,
> *The Vision Forum*
> e-mail newsletter

Children who are educated at home have the unique opportunity to learn and study outside the typical parameters of cookie-cutter curriculum objectives. Instead of being taught what the state or local board of education believes they should know, they learn how to learn. What this means is freedom—freedom to open the mind, explore interests, and become more self-sufficient.

Creativity

Where the confinement of a classroom setting limits opportunities, home-based learning opens a world of creative possibilities. Compare the difference between sitting in a desk all day—where one is trained to start and stop at the sound of a bell—and then learning at home, working at a desirable pace, becoming self-motivated and eventually self-directed. Inspiration requires flexibility. If you've ever been told to do something creative, like write a story or draw a picture, and then you were told you have five minutes to hurry up and finish, you probably know how stifling that can be. Just when the juices start flowing, the bell rings, and it's time to stop. An overstructured, regimented school day is limiting. Creativity blossoms when it is not constricted by a stringent timetable.

Independence

Flexibility and freedom feed not only creativity but independence as well. This means different things for different families, but in large part, homeschooled children eventually learn to be responsible for their own study schedules.

Self-direction and responsibility are critical life skills that carry on into adulthood.

Homeschoolers are often criticized for keeping the apron strings tied too tightly in an effort to overprotect children. Skeptics raise their eyebrows at the notion of overdependent little ones trapped inside a house all day, peering longingly out the window at the outside world. While most homeschoolers would agree that they are selective in choosing their children's outside activities and social settings, they hardly isolate them from society. In actuality, 98 percent of homeschooled students are involved in two or more activities outside the home, which require interaction with various age groups in a variety of settings.[5] These include church activities, sports, the arts, special interest clubs, and volunteer work, to name a few. The scheduling freedom and variety of experiences that round out the home curriculum actually promote a healthier kind of independence than does the highly structured setting of the typical institutional school.

Heightened Educational Standards

As U.S. literacy levels drop and a dumbing-down of education standards continues, home education is a chance to aspire to higher goals of excellence.

As William Butler Yeats said, "Education is not the filling of a bucket but the lighting of a fire." In an educational system where lesson plans rigidly conform to state-controlled objectives, the flames of learning are doused. A fill-in-the-blank approach trains children to merely memorize facts and spit them out on test day. True understanding is sacrificed, and many children are passed along through grade levels without a real grasp on subject matter. Testing standards are then lowered to mask the failure of our school systems, and the downward spiral continues. Homeschooling can raise the bar of learning objectives and tap into the God-given intellectual potential of children.

Proven Track Record

Academically speaking, homeschooling works. But don't take our word for it. Thanks to ongoing research and studies compiled by Dr. Brian Ray of National Home Education Research Institute and others, the statistics speak for themselves.

Test Scores and Grade-level Comparisons

On average, homeschool students consistently outscore their public school peers by 15 to 30 percentile points on standardized achievement tests.[6] Homeschool students in grades one to four generally perform one grade level higher than their public and private school counterparts; and by the eighth grade, the average homeschool student performs four grade levels above the national average.[7] And at the secondary level, homeschoolers score noticeably higher than the national average on SAT and ACT tests, which predict performance in college and universities.[8]

High School Years and College Admissions

Home education has its merits beyond the elementary years. With advanced subjects like physics and calculus in the high school line-up, people may wonder how parents can provide strong educational experiences in areas in which they may not be adept. Homeschoolers have successfully addressed this in a variety of ways. There is a sea of excellent curriculum choices tailored to the needs of homeschoolers, written with parental instruction in mind. Strong self-study skills are usually developed by now, and students often complete courses themselves, with parents overseeing their progress. Another way to pursue the more challenging subjects is through online courses, which provide individualized instruction and evaluation. Many high-school-aged homeschoolers take classes at community colleges, learn through mentorship programs, or participate in co-ops, where families and support groups pool resources and experience. One parent who has a background in art might provide lessons in drawing and painting, while another who is strong in math will offer tutoring in algebra or geometry. When we think outside the box, the possibilities are endless.

Overall, homeschoolers are proving to be well-prepared for college academically, emotionally, and socially. If you're wondering whether your child will be accepted into college with homeschool transcripts, you will be pleased to know that homeschool graduates are highly sought after by many institutions of higher learning. In fact, a number of those holding a homeschool diploma are awarded scholarships. A recent tally showed that more than 750 colleges and universities nationwide are admitting home educated students, and the list is growing extensively.[9] A nationwide survey of college admissions personnel reveals their perception that homeschool graduates show an unusually high occurrence of a key ingredient, which they call "intellectual vitality," and a tendency toward independence and confidence, linked to the developed habits of self-discipline and strong study skills.

> *Why homeschool? Because, above and beyond everything else, you care about the education of your children. In my mind, that's the essence of homeschooling and that's why I tell people that homeschoolers are just like the rest of us, only better.*
>
> WILLIAM BENNETT, former U.S. Secretary of Education

Parental Success as Teachers

And no, you don't have to be a certified teacher to make this happen. Only a small percentage of homeschooling parents have a degree in education, and even then, there is very little difference in performance between certified teachers' families and those where neither parent has a teaching certificate.

Many former teachers, who are now teaching their own at home, take a very different approach to the education of their families. As our family was first embarking on our homeschool journey, these words of wisdom were shared by a homeschool veteran: "Your experience as a classroom teacher may come in handy in some ways, but there will be many things you will need to 'unlearn' as a homeschooling parent." Realizing now the freedom and possibilities that come with learning at home, we would have to agree wholeheartedly.

Parents, you are the professionals of your children. If you love your family and are willing to roll up your sleeves and learn along with them, then no matter what your background, you are qualified to homeschool. There is an abundance of resources available to help you teach your children at home, from curriculum to magazines to Web sites to books. Start with God's Word, and go from there.

Home education is a return to an academically sound form of instruction. More than twenty years since its rebirth, it has proven itself through the bright, competent adults that have grown up in the current movement. From infancy through adulthood, the many benefits to developing minds are only the beginning of the advantages of home education.

Benefits to the Body

Or do you not know that your body is a temple of the
Holy Spirit within you, whom you have from God?
You are not your own, for you were bought with
a price. So glorify God in your body.
1 CORINTHIANS 6:19–20

Physically and socially, children have needs that are best understood and addressed in the loving, nurturing environment of the home. Contrary to a common assumption, children's needs do not diminish as they develop from early childhood into adolescence. The increasing pressures of growing up warrant special parental guidance, attention, and secure family bonds. By following God's original plan, we can bring our children back to the family body to receive the blessings of being nurtured more fully in the home.

Physical Needs

Physically speaking, there are many benefits to educating children at home. We have met families dealing with a variety of special needs related to their children's physical development, and home education proved to be a blessing.

Freedom from Confinement

It is an undeniable fact that children need to move. For those who are especially active, this physical need merges with their mental development. These kinesthetic learners simply learn better by wiggling, touching, and doing. For many children, sitting at a desk for a large portion of the day is torture and usually lands them anywhere from the principal's office to the doctor's office, oftentimes joining the ranks of the medicated.

At home the need for physical activity can be addressed in fun, creative ways. Spelling words are recited while bouncing on the trampoline. Math facts are reviewed by rolling giant dice and moving across a life-size game board through the living room and up the stairway. Nature walks take science lessons and marry them with much needed physical activity. Children learn best by doing, and sometimes that means hopping, skipping, and jumping.

People often ask which room we use for homeschooling, probably picturing straight rows of desks in our living room facing the chalkboard on the wall, and Mrs. Crabtree sitting behind a big desk, with stick in hand. The truth is, these parents don't want to sit behind a desk all day anymore than their children do. Our school is the whole house, the backyard, the bike trails, the museums, the library, and even the grocery store. We read at the breakfast table, on the backyard swing set, on the sofa, and in bed. If classrooms could only be equipped with such comforts.

Special Circumstances

Home education is gaining popularity among families whose children have special needs. Circumstances related to illnesses, handicaps, or learning disabilities warrant a different pace and schedule than that offered by the typical institutional schools.

Studies show that homeschool students with special needs make more academic strides with the one-on-one instruction they would be missing in an institutional setting. At home, children are able to spend more academic time than in a large group setting. Parents are the true experts of their children. Through the support of specialists and networking with other families, they can create a strong learning environment in the home. The joy of experiencing achievements and milestones together is an added "homeroom" bonus for families with special needs children.

> *The potential of any individual is based upon the opportunities presented them.*
> LINDA KANE,
> www.hope-future.org

We recently met a homeschooling mother who spent three years pouring her heart into helping her nine-year-old physically handicapped daughter through six daily hours of therapy. While some of the academics had to be reprioritized, this homeschool family was able to devote time to the child's physical needs without the pressures of a school regimen. As a result, the little girl danced in her first ballet recital, a touching testimony to the blessings of homeschool flexibility, which affords many families like theirs the chance to tailor daily and yearly schedules around special priorities.

In addressing the bodily needs of children, we can also look at aspects related to both intrapersonal and social issues. The question we need to ask ourselves is: Which setting is better for our children—the *student body* or the *family body*?

Socialization

Homeschoolers usually find themselves in a position of having to answer a multitude of queries on how children can be properly educated outside of the typical school setting. But if there's ever one burning question echoing in the ears of homeschoolers, this is it: What about socialization? Perhaps the best answer comes in the form of another question or two: What *is* socialization? And why is the assumption that schools are the best place to socialize children?

Attachment/Detachment

From birth, our babies depend on us for their every need. They do not come with instruction manuals, so we figure out our parental roles as we go. We learn how to comfort them, when to feed them, when they need sleep. As they grow, we understand their cries, their habits, and their unique way of communicating to us. We are there when they learn to walk and speak their first words. We are their teachers from day one, and we love them in a way no one else can.

And then they turn five, or younger in some cases, and we are expected to cut the apron strings and turn them over to the state to continue their education. Some parents do this without batting an eye, accepting it as the norm. For others, it just doesn't feel right. But against strong internal voices, many let go of those little hands that once grasped their own.

The detachment process begins, and almost unknowingly, the gap between child and home widens. Bonds are loosened, and the foundation of trust crumbles. Children, who once looked to their parents for leadership, now turn to their teachers for knowledge, their peers for wisdom, and their music and televisions for entertainment. When the fabric of the family loses its intended purpose and strength, children are at greater risk of being lost to the world.

This has become the unquestioned norm in our society, and the unfortunate consequence is an epidemic of fragmented families. By reevaluating the traditional methods of socializing children, parents can choose a course that makes more sense.

By one definition, *socialization* means: "To fit for companionship with others;" or "to make sociable in attitude or manners."[1] Where companionship, attitude, manners, and relationships are concerned, it is important to examine the distinct ramifications of socializing children in various settings throughout their lives.

Diversity over Segregation

One of many negative aspects of school socialization is the unnatural environment of age-segregation. As stated by John Taylor Gatto, 1990 New York City Teacher of the Year, "It is absurd and anti-life to be part of a system that compels you to sit in confinement with people of exactly the same age and social class. That system effectively cuts you off from the immense diversity of life and the synergy of variety."[2]

With younger and older siblings, mothers and fathers, grandparents and extended families, friends and neighbors, pastors and piano teachers, homeschool families have plenty of opportunities to experience rich social variety. Homeschool schedules often include volunteer work, community service, church activities, and local and international missions trips, encouraging children to look beyond the self. Field trips and family travels expose them to different cultures and provide opportunities to appreciate the world at large. The notion that homeschooling cuts children off from the real world is a myth. It is the social segregation and isolation of the institutionalized masses that should be cause for concern.

Folly

When fitting our children for companionship with others, what is an appropriate environment? In the large-group setting of conventional schools, there is typically one overextended teacher attempting to govern a crowd of impressionable children. Like the blind leading the blind, much of the shepherding is done by the children them-selves. As the book of Proverbs points out, this is neither wise nor prudent: "Folly is bound up in the heart of a child . . ." (Proverbs 22:15).

In other words, children, naturally born into sin, are naturally prone to foolishness. Does it make sense to put a bunch of children together all day, five days a week—children whose hearts are bound by folly? If we want to train up our children to act in a socially acceptable way, they should spend their formative years with people who act socially acceptable. How do you define social acceptability? Our guess is that it would not match up with much of the behavior you would see in educational institutions.

The deterioration of our culture is gradual, but when noting the downward spiral of discipline problems in schools, one can see how far we have actually sunk. Forty to fifty years ago, public school teachers indicated on surveys that the biggest discipline problems in classrooms were tardiness, talkative students, and gum chewing.[3] Today, the list of complaints made by teachers, administrators, and students has grown to include the ever-increasing presence of drugs, gangs, and weapons on school grounds, and the threat of assault, robbery, theft, vandalism, and rape.[4]

> [Folly] is in the heart of children; they bring it into the world with them; it is what they were conceived in. It is not only found there, but it is bound there . . . it is true of ourselves . . . it is true of our children, whom we have begotten in our own likeness.
>
> MATTHEW HENRY

If you think this kind of violence is limited to inner-city high schools, consider a recent report: "Elementary school principals and safety experts say they're seeing more violence and aggression than ever among their youngest students, pointing to what they see as an alarming rise in assaults and threats to classmates and teachers. 'Some of my most violent kids have been in kindergarten, first and second grade,' an elementary school principal in rural Wisconsin says. 'They simply lose control, and it comes out in extremely violent manners.'"[5]

Parents must really evaluate where their children spend the majority of their time. Let's look at the statistics. After thirty-five to forty hours a week in classrooms and in transit to and from school, topped off by additional hours of nightly homework per week, extracurricular or peer-related activities, and three to five hours of daily television viewing on average, there is very little time left for family interaction. The home, where the majority of values should be imparted, has been reduced to a pit stop, with little meaningful parental contact. The best hours of the day are spent under the influence of other people, most of whom parents of institutional school children have little or no say in selecting. Believe it or not, a recent nationwide U.S. study found that 40 percent of fathers do not even know the names of their childrens' teachers.[6] This is a startling prospect considering the impact a teacher can make on a young, pliable mind.

Peer Dependence

Parents often rationalize, "But my children want to go to school. They like being with their friends. . . ." That may be so. The question these parents need to ask themselves is—when and how do children develop this appetite? Perhaps it is from previous years of being plucked out of the nest and left in the care of another. Many parents instigate peer dependence by smothering their schedules with too many outside activities. Children's wants do not necessarily reflect their needs. Most children want candy for breakfast, lunch, and dinner. They would love to play computer games all day. When parents lack discernment and fail to guide their children according to their real needs, children choose for themselves.

Research shows that when the school bell rings, students are typically more inclined to spend additional time with peer groups by choice rather than with parents or siblings. One mother expressed her amazement that after being in school all day with her friends, her daughter would spend another two hours gabbing with them on the phone. Internet chat rooms, instant messaging, and e-mail add further enticement to peer dependence. There's nothing wrong with enjoying friendships, but there are consequences to spending a disproportionate amount of time with peers over parents. Considering where our culture is today, it can be a recipe for disaster.

When impressionable children and teens live under the strong influence of one another, spiritual and emotional immaturity take root and the craving for worldly things often grows. This can be seen today—the desire to fit in physically through immodest attire, sexual impurity, substance abuse, materialism, and all the fleshy temptations that are constantly flashed in front of the eyes of youth. Once this appetite is established, it is difficult to control or change. Again, wisdom's warning can be found in Scripture: "Whoever walks with the wise becomes wise, but the companion of fools will suffer harm" (Proverbs 13:20).

The attitudes of young people reflect a growing rebellion toward authority and a self-centered view of the world. By removing our children's bodies from the safety and sanity of their home and thrusting them into this kind of scenario, they become easy prey for Satan, who works to corrupt the body of Christ.

Family Values

Homeschooling is not just about social skills. It's about building relationships. By fostering family togetherness, homeschooling strengthens bonds between children and their parents and siblings. In fact, one of the top five reasons parents cite for homeschooling is building strong family ties. According to research, these families have about 53 percent more time available to be together than those whose children are sent away from home to institutional schools.[7] This explains why home educated children generally perceive their parents as primary authority figures more often than do public and private school children. Also, siblings are often best friends instead of archrivals, and children are not embarrassed to be with their families. The majority of home educated students who are now adults emphasize the importance of family, saying they are glad their parents educated them and would recommend it to others.

> I would encourage each of you to take advantage of the friends God has placed in your very home.
>
> JESSICA ERBER, homeschooler

Our culture is steeped in moral relativism. Whose values do you want your children to embrace? Public schools have taken the liberty to indoctrinate children with perverse ideas of masculine and feminine roles. It is no longer a given that little girls will grow up to exemplify virtuous womanhood and little boys true manhood. Parents must be deliberate about teaching children how to make choices in light of

Scripture, that they may glorify God in their future calling in the church, the workplace, and the family.

In today's do-whatever-feels-good society, the biblical model of the family is at stake. In the Christian household, fathers have more opportunities to train their sons up to be godly leaders, and to demonstrate what it means to love their wives as Christ loved the church (see Ephesians 5:25). Working alongside their mothers, daughters can learn the virtues of femininity and the noble calling of being keepers at home. They witness firsthand the joy of being suitable helpmates to their husbands (see Genesis 2:18). At home, the foundations of the biblical family are made stronger.

The Common Good

Contrary to a common misconception that homeschoolers are withdrawing from public life, or hurting the common good, research confirms that the society at large benefits from the home education movement. Besides strengthening the family institution, most homeschool families are very politically conscious and are involved in activities such as community service, membership in local organizations, and voting. The long-term effects of civic involvement and service to the community are now visible, as individuals who were home educated are proving to carry these practices into adulthood.

The general public benefits from homeschooling in yet another way: financially. Home education is more cost-effective than public or private education. The median amount families spend per child taught at home is $450, which includes books, extra-curricular classes, and field trips.[8] Compare that to today's price tag of nearly $7,000 per student in the institutional schools. The total K–12 federal, state, and local spending for education, both public and private, climbed to more than $420 billion for the 2000–2001 school year.[9]

The benefits of properly educated children will be felt by generations to come. If our goal is to raise respectable and contributing members of society, upholding the basic freedoms and moral principles upon which this land was established, we must teach them to look beyond the self.

> *Home education families are not dependent on public, tax-funded resources. They likely save American taxpayers over $10 billion per year.*
>
> DR. BRIAN RAY,
> National Home
> Education Research
> Institute

If we truly want our children to be active members of the body of Christ, we must socialize them in an atmosphere that nurtures rather than corrupts.

Body of Christ

Ultimately, the goal of Christian parents is to disciple our children and encourage them to love the Lord with all their hearts, minds, and souls, and to love their neighbors as themselves, that they may become productive members of the Body of Christ. When each one is strong in his role, he can then carry forth the plan God has designed specifically for him.

Soldiers in Training

As Christians, our purpose is to be out there as soldiers of the cross. But our children must first be fully armed with the truth before they can be sent into the battle. Home education can provide solid basic training for God's future army.

The Lord can and should be woven into our curriculum constantly. He is the Lord of all matters of the mind—science, history, language, math, and the arts—not just an isolated religion class. State curriculum not only ignores this, it indoctrinates against it. There is no such thing as a neutral education. Either deliberately or unknowingly, a philosophy or set of values will be imparted. When parents acknowledge this and fulfill their duty to teach their children diligently, they are outfitting them with the full armor of God. In so doing, they are enabling them to rise up when they are mature in Christ and carry out His battle plan with strength and wisdom.

> *There is no neutral ground in the universe: every square inch, every split second is claimed by God and counter-claimed by Satan.*
>
> C. S. LEWIS, "Christianity and Culture"

Salt and Light

A popular argument for putting Christian kids in public schools is to be salt and light in an unbelieving world. Is it realistic to expect a first grader, a preadolescent, or even a teenager to sprinkle salt or shed light prematurely? How does a child go out and make disciples of all nations before he even has a firm grip on the Word of God? Just as we do not transplant a seedling before it develops strong roots, it doesn't make sense to thrust children into a role that requires spiritual maturity.

Consider Jesus' words, "Salt is good, but if salt has lost its taste, how shall its saltiness be restored? It is of no use either for the soil or for the manure pile. It is thrown away. He who has ears to hear, let him hear" (Luke 14:34–35).

Not only is it unwise to send children as missionaries to public schools, which are often adamantly opposed to Christian doctrine, it is dangerous as well. How effectively can impressionable youth stand up for biblical principles in a place where the state has injected curriculum with the lies of humanism, evolution, and twisted ideas of marriage and family, and where labels like "intolerant" and "narrow-minded" are thrown at anyone who stands up for the truth? If children were truly expected to reach the lost in public schools, which seems contradictory to Scripture, then there would be more evidence of fruitfulness. To the contrary, we hear more and more instances of children with "good morals" being corrupted by "bad company" (see 1 Corinthians 15:33), and the consequences are devastating. Studies are indicating that most Christian children in the public schools are not gaining converts— they are rejecting Christ.

As skeptical as people are about homeschooling as it relates to socialization, this is really one of the most convicting reasons that families are bringing their children home, where parents have more say in who influences their children. Unless these influences line up with the Word of God, not only are their bodies at risk, so are their souls.

> *With over 90 percent of Christian youth holding to Secular Humanism views rather than to Biblical Theism views, the future of the church in America appears troubling.*
>
> DAN SMITHWICK,
> President, Nehemiah
> Institute

Benefits to the Soul

*And the Lord God formed man of the dust
of the ground, and breathed into his nostrils the breath of
life; and man became a living soul.*

GENESIS 2:7 (KJV)

Educational philosophies and goals, as varied as they may be, usually have one common thread: *shaping the future of the student.* From a state objective, future goals usually center on the student's contribution to a social agenda, producing a citizen who serves to further the goals of the state. From a more self-focused point of view, personal success and worldly achievement are typically the aim, producing a person who lives to serve himself. But from a Christian perspective, man's ultimate purpose is to serve and glorify God. So in the education of children, the term *future* takes on a whole new meaning—our sole purpose becomes a soul purpose.

Eternal Perspective

Eternity—it's hard for the mind to even fathom the infinite, the timeless. But the choices we make today in shaping our children's future can lead them down the path of their eternal destination, as well as that of their children and their children's children. We cannot think of a greater responsibility and privilege as parents.

As Scripture reminds us, "What is your life? For you are a mist that appears for a little time and then vanishes" (James 4:14). Our time here on earth is just a blink of an eye compared to the eternity that awaits us hereafter. We can choose to spend our time chasing personal goals, dreams, and possessions, to go with the flow and use the excuse "I turned out OK." Or we can be a willing servant and, as the apostle Paul said, "press on toward the goal for the prize of the upward call of God in Christ Jesus" (Philippians 3:14).

Our "upward call" is to be prudent in the vital task of parenthood. Our children are actually His children, a gift to us for the purpose of bringing up "in the discipline and instruction of the Lord" (Ephesians 6:4). We will stand before our Maker one day and be held accountable for what we have done to accomplish the greatest task we as parents have here on earth—a task with an everlasting impact.

Firm Foundation

Our children's lives reflect their beliefs, and their beliefs are built upon what they have been taught. The absence of biblical teaching in the home has proven to contribute to the growing problem of biblical illiteracy in the Christian community. Many professing Christians cannot identify more than two or three of the disciples, and 60 percent cannot name even five of the Ten Commandments.[1]

Too many Christians have become complacent in their preschool-level of Bible understanding. While claiming that the gospel is at the core of their beliefs, many are failing to apply its principles to their lives. As a result, the Church has witnessed a severe compromise of standards and behavior, which ultimately nullifies a Christian's testimony. The responsibility of spiritual training belongs to the parents and must be a priority in every home. While the church may provide assistance, Sunday school and youth programs should never be a substitute for the instruction that God has commanded to be carried out first and foremost within the family.

> *Americans revere the Bible—but, by and large, they don't read it. And because they don't read it, they have become a nation of biblical illiterates.*
>
> GEORGE GALLUP AND JIM CASTELLI, *The People's Religion*

Wise and Foolish Builders

Jesus' Parable of the Wise and Foolish Builders (see Matthew 7:24–27) demonstrates our need to build foundations upon the rock of God's principles. In training up our children, it takes time to build these foundations. "When you rise up and when you lie down," the Bible says (Deuteronomy 6:7). Public schools are built upon the sinking sand of false ideologies and unbiblical agendas—not neutral, but anti-God agendas. It is dangerous to assume that a weekly Sunday school class or youth social event will undo the fifty or more hours that children spend in state institutions where they are influenced by ideas that blatantly contradict God's Word.

Would it be prudent to expect our children's physical health to thrive if they ate candy all week and we threw in a tossed green salad on Sunday morning? Of course it wouldn't. But this is the kind of spiritual diet partaken by many children of born-again Christian families.

> *Education is thus a most powerful ally of humanism,*
> *and every American school is a school of humanism.*
> *What can a theistic Sunday school's meeting for an hour once a*
> *week and teaching only a fraction of the children do to stem*
> *the tide of the five-day program of humanistic teaching?*
>
> CHARLES POTTER, *Humanism: A New Religion*

A recent Barna Group poll reveals some disturbing information. In a survey of parents across America, research shows that there is a lack of difference in the way born-again Christian parents and their non-believing counterparts are raising their children. In fact, born-again Christian parents partaking in the study were more likely to put an emphasis on seeing that their children received a good education over seeing them become followers of Christ. Among other areas of importance to these parents were helping children feel secure, affirmed, encouraged, happy. Only three out of ten Christian parents even included the salvation of their child in the list. George Barna explains:

> Believers do not train their children to think or act any differently. When our kids are exposed to the same influences, without much supervision, and are generally not guided to interpret their circumstances and opportunities in light of biblical principles, it's no wonder that they grow up to be just as involved in gambling, adultery, divorce, cohabitation, excessive drinking and other unbiblical behaviors as everyone else.[2]

Make no mistake—our children will be tested. They will have to withstand temptation and weather the storms of life ahead. The time we spend with them now in fervent prayer and preparation will not be in vain. Be sure they truly know, fully understand, and passionately embrace the principles of Christ, the Solid Rock.

Wisdom

Jesus contrasted the two builders as being wise and foolish. Let's talk about *wise* and what that means in educating our families. The Bible gives us many good passages about wisdom, including its foundation: a fear of the Lord. "The fear of the LORD is the beginning of wisdom; all those who practice it have a good understanding" (Psalm 111:10). Fearing the Lord—respect, honor, reverence, awe, and yes, even healthy fear for His unsurpassed holiness compared to our complete inadequacy, our utter doom without Him—this is the beginning, and foundation, to our goal in training up our children. Every day should be an opportunity for us to say "Come, O children, listen to me; I will teach you the fear of the LORD" (Psalm 34:11).

In the world's eyes, wisdom is measured through academic intelligence or material success. In God's eyes, true wisdom comes from following the principles He has laid out for us in Scripture. These very principles should be the backbone of our teaching. What is worldly wisdom apart from Christ?

> *By wisdom a house is built, and by understanding it is established.*
> PROVERBS 24:3

Heart and Mind

When leading our children to the Lord, it helps to understand the foundations of true wisdom and learning. Most of the scientific theories on learning are based solely on the mind or the body. In behaviorism, for example, man is viewed as a personless body, and research is based on the study of laboratory animals. Pavlov and Skinner were behaviorists, famous for their studies on rats and dogs. The science of humanism views man as a biological organism, using people as the basis of its research. It focuses on man's achievements, purporting that knowledge exists in its own right, devoid of any reference to God. As pointed out earlier, the ideas of humanism and evolution were central to the founding of our current education system.

Both the behaviorist "man is animal" theory and the humanist "up with man, down with God" mind-set are infused into the public education system. Learning that is Bible-based, however, views man in the image of God, rooted in the understanding that true knowledge and wisdom come from the Creator, who inspires the heart and mind.

Knowing that we have been created in God's image with eternal souls causes Christians to look at learning from a different angle. The heart (or soul) is involved, and that idea becomes the springboard for teaching our children. In other words, education can be geared toward manipulating masses of students toward a worldly agenda, training children much like Pavlov trained his dogs, to mechanically react at the sound of a bell, or perform for an external reward. Like humanists, the focus could be personal achievement, such as passing the test, making the grade, climbing the ladder of recognition, and "grabbing the gusto." Or, Scripture can be the basis for learning, appealing to the hearts of children, and instilling in them a desire to "work heartily as for the Lord" (Colossians 3:23).

The underlying purpose of training up children should be obedience to God's commands, even when their rebellious nature drives them to do the opposite. We are commanded to obey, out of fear (the beginning of wisdom) and love, for all that God has first done for us. All of these ideas stem from the heart, which is clearly linked to the development of the mind. When the heart is rightly motivated, a fire is lit to explore, work diligently, and ultimately follow God's path for our lives.

Education expert Dr. Ruth Beechick explains the correlation between our hearts and our minds, or the way we think and learn. She says, "On the motivation side of the learning model, heart is deeply involved. Conscience, will, purpose, and determination . . . as being associated with the heart, play their part in learning. They must be part of a biblical theory of learning."[3]

As this relates to homeschooling, Dr. Beechick continues:

> Parents . . . have achieved remarkable results in their teaching. For the most part they have lacked formal teacher training, yet their results far outstrip the results of our government schooling institutions. This has to be due to the heart-to-heart approach that parents naturally use with their children. They use any curriculum or no curriculum;

they use popular methods or homemade methods; yet they overwhelmingly produce superior results.[4]

Our children may or may not be gifted with the mathematical skill to become engineers, the scientific knowledge to become brain surgeons, or the mastery of language to become best-selling authors. But if they love and fear the Lord, learn to love Jesus as their Lord and Savior, and live to serve Him in whatever area to which they are called, while embracing Scripture as their roadmap throughout life, then we have done our job as imparters of true wisdom.

Treasures

It has been said that our checkbooks reveal where our treasure is. It is also fair to say that our daily calendars also reflect where our passions and priorities lie. What we sow now, in time, money, and energy, will surely impact that which we and our families will reap later.

> There is no such thing as values-free education. With the banning of Christian values and their replacement with humanistic ones in the public school system, we have witnessed the adoption of bizarre ideas having little to do with academics and everything to do with social engineering, directly resulting, ultimately, in the corruption of educational quality.
>
> DAVID LIMBAUGH,
> *WorldNet Daily*

Time and Priorities

Jesus said, "For where your treasure is, there your heart will be also" (Matthew 6:21). The sacrifice of time and material things made by parents who choose the path of home education tells children they are the treasures in their parents' hearts. Oftentimes, this means a second income is sacrificed so that mom can stay home. But families find creative ways to

> *I have no greater joy than to hear that my children are walking in the truth.*
>
> 3 JOHN 4

make ends meet, and you cannot put a price on the message that your family's well-being is a priority.

What will children remember most—that they had all the latest toys, the coolest clothes, and the biggest house on the block, or that their parents were there when they needed them most? In the final analysis, the parents who sacrificed the temporal for the eternal will have a greater satisfaction and joy.

Developing Passion through Obedience

It is important to note that parents usually develop an even stronger passion for their role as mothers and fathers when they are involved in their children's education. Did you ever notice that the more you know about something, the more interesting it becomes? The same holds true for parents and their children. The more time we spend with them, taking part in their activities and sharing their interests, the more intimately we know them and the greater our desire grows to embrace this brief time we share together.

By contrast, how often have we heard frazzled mothers during the first few weeks (or days) of summer vacation longing for the start of the next school year? This is heartbreaking. It may be easier when the children are out of mom's hair, but in the end, is it more rewarding?

Some people say to us, "I could never homeschool. I just don't have the patience or the discipline." Perhaps the true sentiment behind those statements lies in the lack of desire or interest. Yes, it is a sacrifice. Yes, there are days when a homeschool parent would just like to be left alone. But no other activity, be it that much-needed workout at the gym, the lunch date with friends, or your favorite television shows, can take higher priority than that of raising godly children.

We have also heard the comment "Well sure, you were meant to homeschool your children. I guess it's a calling." All parents are called to choose wisely the best path for training and discipling their children. Many have simply lost sight of what that path looks like. By really tuning into Scripture and closely examining their options, perhaps more parents will hear that voice calling their names as well.

> *Choose this day whom you will serve . . . but as for me and my house, we will serve the Lord.*
> JOSHUA 24:15

Are you being called to this purpose? Are you listening to that voice, or are you letting the demons of doubt and a hundred distractions pull you away from the cause of rising up in the home education movement? If you are among the doubters, our advice to you is this: respond obediently to the Lord and trust that He will provide you with the passion and tools to do the job. Don't use a lack of character or confidence as an excuse.

If patience was a prerequisite, only a fraction of current homeschoolers would be doing it today. If doubt or disinterest always dictated our decision-making in life, what would that say about our faith? Let God transform you into the parent He wants you to be. Every opportunity to serve and obey Him is an opportunity to grow. Turn your hearts toward your children, and you will experience the blessings of a continuously deepening love and commitment to them.

Lasting Legacy

In *A Biblical Vision for Multi-Generational Faithfulness*, William Einwechter shares this wisdom:

> If a man wants to change the world for generations to come, let him look well to his duties in the family, and be the means of continuing or beginning, as the case may be a dynasty of God-honoring, Christ-serving, kingdom-advancing children, grandchildren, great grandchildren. . . . The potential impact for the glory of God and the advance

of His kingdom is exponential for the Christian family. The future belongs to families that exhibit multi-generational faithfulness and fruitfulness![5]

Amen! Christianity is under attack, and the institutions of public education turn out more and more casualties every year. Whether one chooses to acknowledge this or merely be sidetracked by life's many diversions, our children are easy prey to those who are working tooth and nail to subvert moral and biblical standards that were once widely accepted by generations past. The effort we put forth now to train up followers of Christ can and most certainly will affect the future of His body of believers. Are you being called to this purpose? The actions that we take today will have a lasting impact for generations to come.

> But the steadfast love of the LORD is from everlasting to everlasting on those who fear him, and his righteousness to children's children.
> PSALM 103:17

Our little reasons for choosing the path of homeschooling have become big reasons. The list of blessings that the Lord has bestowed upon us grows longer each year, and our convictions continue to become stronger. Next to our faith and our marriage, taking the path of home education has been the most rewarding part of our lives. We simply cannot imagine doing it any other way.

Those same blessings are available to all who are willing to receive. Picture our heavenly Father above, waiting to shower upon us those blessings until our cups overflow with more goodness than we ever expected. And all we have to do is say, "We love you, Lord. And we will follow."

Jesus answered him, "If anyone loves me, he will keep my word, and my Father will love him, and we will come to him and make our home with him. Whoever does not love me does not keep my words. And the word that you hear is not mine but the Father's who sent me."

JOHN 14:23–24

Afterword

*For I know the plans I have for you, declares
the* LORD, *plans for wholeness and not for evil,
to give you a future and a hope.*

JEREMIAH 29:11

To homeschool is to take a step on a narrow path. Jesus encourages us to "enter by the narrow gate. For the gate is wide and the way is easy that leads to destruction, and those who enter by it are many" (Matthew 7:13). More and more are finding this path, but homeschooling is still considered countercultural. Prepare to face skepticism, even criticism, not just by unbelievers, but by fellow Christians as well. Your neighbors may raise their eyebrows, school personnel may question your qualifications, and your mother-in-law may even tell you that you are going to ruin her grandchildren. In time, the blessings and fruit will speak for themselves: happy, well-adjusted (and yes, well-socialized) children who are not only smart but wise; close-knit families; and the joy and peace that come from being obedient to God's Word.

The proof will be in the pudding, as the saying goes. But the bottom line is this—you will be held accountable before your children's Creator. He has entrusted to you the care of His lambs, to nurture their minds, bodies, and souls. This is a task and privilege we must take seriously, for the results will have an everlasting impact. Pray fervently and ask for the heavenly Father's guidance in your decision. With Him on your side, you can move forward with confidence and joy. If you're not sure what your first step should be, the following ideas will help you get started.

Get on the same page. In order for there to be family harmony, there must be unity between husband and wife. It will be a very stressful, unhealthy homeschool environment if the parents are not united in this endeavor. Biblically speaking, if the husband, the head of the household, is not in agreement with the decision to homeschool, the wife must graciously submit. A wife should bring it to the Lord, and if it is His will, He will be the one to turn the husband's heart toward his children. "But I want you to understand that the head of every man is Christ, the head of a wife is her husband, and the head of Christ is God" (1 Corinthians 11:3).

Get on your knees. I (Kim) remember waking up in the middle of the night, my heart racing, thinking about all that lay ahead of us. Like the night before a big trip, my mind was constantly sorting through everything I needed to do to prepare, knowing that we were about to embark on one of the greatest adventures of our lives. Praying gave me peace, guidance, and reassurance. Panic turned to excitement as we planned for our new journey ahead. "Trust in the LORD with all your heart, and do not lean on your own understanding. In all your ways acknowledge him, and he will make straight your paths" (Proverbs 3:5–6).

Get in the Word. The Bible is our instruction manual in life. If God's Word doesn't convict you, nothing else—no book, magazine article, or friendly advice—will. As pointed out in Scripture, "The word of God is living and active" (Hebrews 4:12) and "will stand forever" (Isaiah 40:8). In order for us to be effective teachers to our children, we must go to the Teacher for instruction on a regular basis ourselves. "Your word is a lamp to my feet and a light to my path" (Psalm 119:105).

Get connected. Find other homeschoolers in your area that you can connect with. Most state homeschool organizations have Web sites that can lead you to local support groups. There are many great forums on the Internet with discussion boards, links to suppliers, and idea exchanges. Talk to homeschool veterans. They are happy to offer wisdom and encouragement. "Therefore encourage one another and build one another up, just as you are doing" (1 Thessalonians 5:11).

Get inspired. Attend your state homeschool convention. The workshops and keynote speakers will provide inspiration and how-to for beginners and experienced alike. Just being among so many like-minded parents is encouraging. Most conventions include an array of vendor tables, which give you the opportunity to explore books and products, compare materials, and ask questions before making purchases. "Ask, and it will be given to you; seek, and you will find; knock, and it will be opened to you" (Matthew 7:7).

Get acquainted. There are many methods of homeschooling and a huge assortment of curriculum companies from which to choose. Find out which style fits best with your vision of homeschooling and your family's needs. You may find that you like a little from each, and wish to build your own eclectic approach. Catalogs are a great way to get your arms around the various methods and materials available. "Seek first the kingdom of God and his righteousness, and all these things will be added to you" (Matthew 6:33).

Get acclimated. If your children have been in the institutional school setting for a while, it is wise to allow for some "decompression time" before jumping into home studies. Some people have suggested taking a month of readjustment time for each year children have been in school. During this period, reconnect with your children. Share goals, dreams, and ideas for your educational journey together. Get to know their learning styles and interests. And don't forget to lay the groundwork for your expectations in areas such as behavior, attitude, and household responsibilities. Character issues must not be overshadowed by academics. With the groundwork in place, you will be ready for a strong start and and even stronger finish. "And he will turn the hearts of fathers to their children and the hearts of children to their fathers" (Malachi 4:6).

Get a vision. Establishing a vision and goals for your family is an important part of determining your path and evaluating your progress. It also serves as a tool for choosing curriculum and making schedules. If something doesn't fit in with your plan and purpose, scratch it. Reassess what works and what doesn't, and be flexible with your plans. As your children grow and change, each year will be a little different. Like a journey into the unknown, you will discover new and exciting things along the way that will surprise and delight you. "Commit your work to the LORD, and your plans will be established" (Proverbs 16:3).

Blessings on your journey!

Notes

History

1. Edwin G. West, "The Spread of Education Before Compulsion: Britain and America in the Nineteenth Century" published in *The Freeman: Ideas on Liberty* (July 1996).
2. Irwin S. Kirsch, Ann Jungelblut, Lynn Jenkins, and Andrew Kolstad, "Executive Summary of Adult Literacy in America: A First Look at the Results of the National Adult Literacy Survey," (nces.ed.gov) National Center for Education Statistics, http://nces.ed.gov/naal/resources/execsumm.asp (accessed July 29, 2005).
3. John Taylor Gatto, *The Underground History of American Education: A Schoolteacher's Intimate Investigation Into the Problem of Modern Schooling* (New York: The Oxford Village Press, 2000), 54.
4. Alan Caruba, "Illiterate America" Thought You Should Know-TYSK, www.tysknews.com/Depts/Educate/illiterate_america.htm (accessed July 29, 2005).
5. Christopher Klicka, *Homeschooling: The Right Choice* (Nashville: Broadman & Holman Publishers, 2002), 162.
6. Ibid., 162.
7. N. C. Gillespie, from a letter to Asa Gray, Harvard biology professor, cited in "Charles Darwin and the Problem of Creation," www.talkorigins.org/faqs/quotes/mine/part2.html (accessed July 29, 2005).
8. Dr. Brian Ray, *2004–2005 Worldwide Guide to Homeschooling* (Nashville: Broadman & Holman Publishers, 2004), 27.
9. Ibid., 7–8.
10. Ibid., 28.
11. Ibid., 42.
12. Klicka, *Homeschooling: The Right Choice*, 102.

Mind

1. Dr. Raymond and Dorothy Moore, "When Education Becomes Abuse: A Different Look at the Mental Health of Children," The Moore Foundation and Academy, www.moorefoundation.com/When%20Education%20Becomes%20Abuse.html (accessed July 29, 2005).
2. Linda Kane, "The Neurodevelopmental Approach to Development," *The Alliant, Illinois Christian Home Educators*, (Summer 2005), 22.
3. Alan Caruba, "Illiterate America," Thought You Should Know-TYSK, www.tysknews.com/Depts/Educate/illiterate_America.htm (accessed July 29, 2005).
4. Ibid.
5. Ray, *2004–2005 Worldwide Guide to Homeschooling*, 59.
6. Ibid., 48.
7. Lawrence Rudner "Scholastic Achievement and Demographic Characteristics of Home School Students," (Summary of Major Findings—Achievement) Education Policy Analysis Archives, http://epaa.asu.edu/epaa/v7n8 (accessed July 29, 2005).
8. Ray, *2004–2005 Worldwide Guide to Homeschooling*, 69.
9. Ibid., 70.

Body

1. *The American Heritage Dictionary of the English Language*, New College ed. (Boston: Houghton Mifflin, 1984), 1225.
2. John Taylor Gatto, Teacher of the Year Acceptance Speech, January 31, 1990, www.quaqua.org/Gattoteach.htm (accessed July 29, 2005).
3. Dennis Jay Kenney and Steuart Watson, "Crime in the Schools: Reducing Conflict with Student Problem Solving," *National Institute of Justice; Research in Brief* (July 1999).
4. Ibid.
5. Greg Toppo, "School Violence Hits Lower Grades," *USA Today*, January 13, 2004.
6. Ray, *2004–2005 Worldwide Guide to Homeschooling*, 107.
7. Ibid.
8. Ibid., 38.
9. Krista Kafer, "Education Statistics" *The Heritage Foundation, Policy Research and Analysis*, www.heritage.org/Research/Education/wm134.cfm (accessed July 29, 2005).

Soul

1. Albert Mohler, "The Scandal of Biblical Illiteracy: It's Our Problem," Crosswalk Weblogs, www.goshen.com/faith/1218766.html (accessed July 29, 2005).
2. George Barna, "The Barna Update: Parents Describe How They Raise Their Children," www.barna.org/FlexPage.aspx?Page=Barna Update&BarnaUpdateID=183 (accessed July 29, 2005).
3. Dr. Ruth Beechick, *Heart & Mind—What the Bible Says About Learning* (Fenton, MI: Mott Media, 2004), 52.
4. Ibid., 5–6.
5. William Einwechter, *A Biblical Vision for Multi-Generational Faithfulness*, CD, Vision Forum, www.visionforum.com.

Recommended Resources

The Harsh Truth About Public Schools
Bruce Shortt

Heart & Mind—What the Bible Says about Learning
Dr. Ruth Beechick

Home Educated and Now Adults
Brian D. Ray, Ph.D.

Homeschooling: The Right Choice
Christopher J. Klicka

*Millstones & Stumbling Blocks—Understanding Education in
  Post-Christian America*
Bradley Heath

The Underground History of American Education
John Taylor Gatto

Worldwide Guide to Homeschooling
Brian D. Ray, Ph.D.

Homeschool Digest
www.homeschooldigest.com

The Old Schoolhouse Magazine
www.theoldschoolhouse.com

Answers In Genesis
www.answersingenesis.org

Christian Homeschool Fellowship
www.chfweb.net

Dexios
www.dexios.info

Exodus Mandate
www.exodusmandate.com

Home School Legal Defense Association
www.hslda.com

Homeschooling Family to Family
www.homeschoolingfamilytofamily.org

National Home Education Research Institute
www.nheri.org

Vision Forum
www.visionforum.com